We Have Voices

The **Methodist** Church

methodist.org.uk
Registered charity no. 1132208

First published 2024 by the Methodist Church in Great Britain

ISBN 978-1-85852-525-9

Printed and bound by Short Run Press Ltd, Exeter

We Have **Voices**

Praying together for
peace, justice and change

Edited by Barbara Glasson

The **Methodist** Church

Contents

Introduction	1
Lament	4
Solidarity	24
Courage	42
Sending	74
A Simple Pattern of Prayer	86
About the Editor	89
Contributors	90

Introduction

Our desire for justice is hard to put into words. It comes from deep within the human soul. We long for things to be different – and yet often feel powerless to make effective change.

How can we tackle inequality and poverty and seek life in all its fullness for all people? How can we act justly in relation to environmental pressures that seem so vast and beyond our control? How can we seek justice for refugees and asylum seekers who are displaced by war and economic pressures but whose names are unknown to us? How may we, as small human people who seek to follow Jesus, oppose discrimination and see all people made in the image of God? Against seemingly overwhelming odds how is it possible to oppose warfare and promote our deepest longings for reconciliation? Our desire for justice brings a quandary of questions that in turn can cause a tsunami of helplessness.

Yet, and even so, we are people who are called and committed to transformation and hopefulness, and however small and silent we may feel, we have voices! We have voices to cry out against injustice, we have voices to speak for and with others, we have voices to rail at God and confide in God, we have voices to tell truth to power. So what is this hope and how do we discern the difference between Christian hope and banal wishful thinking?

One approach to these perplexing questions is the recognition that, while this calling is an individual one, it is also – and most importantly – collective: we are called to transformative hope together and to voice our vison of a more just world together. Our faith communities may feel fragile and challenged, but as we gather together in chapel or church they remind us always that we are not alone. Each week we are in communion with Christians around the world who through action and prayer gather to bring their longings to God and are inspired by the Holy Spirit both to speak out and to roll up their sleeves to bring about the kingdom for which Jesus died. Our hope is in the community of prayer and company of witnesses within which we play our small but mighty part, to which we add our voice.

The 2023 Methodist Conference adopted the 'Justice-seeking Church' report, along with six Principles for justice, namely:

- God made humans in the image of God, each worthy of equal value and dignity
- God desires the flourishing of creation and human community within it
- God has shown a bias to people experiencing poverty and those who are excluded
- God entrusts those in power with special responsibilities for upholding justice
- God calls all people and nations actively to work for peace and justice, liberation and transformation
- God calls us to live in hope and in ways that reflect God's character and the pattern of God's kingdom.

These principles show that 'doing justice' is not simply another agenda item, but rather that our calling means that justice needs to be embedded within every aspect of Christian living.

In the pages that follow are prayers and meditations that a number of individuals have written for use in collective worship. With considerable trepidation each person has risen to the challenge of gleaning and sifting words to describe their longing for justice, peace and reconciliation. This collection shares the voices of a wide and diverse range of people, from as far away as South America and Myanmar and as close by as the local foodbank. We hear from army chaplains, young people working in community projects and older people who faithfully long to see justice for all. These are some of the voices that in different tongues and accents add to a collective clamour for peace and justice.

This resource is both to be taken off the shelf on a Sunday morning for leading worship, and in the week for reminding us that our longing for justice is not only a future hope but a current and collective responsibility.

It is divided into four main sections: Lament, Solidarity, Courage and Sending, which provide a liturgical 'flow' to the contents. There is a short example of a simple form of worship at the end of the book. While we hope this will be helpful for people who lead worship, it is not prescriptive and we encourage you to play with the words, enabling your voices to express the impetus for justice we are seeking to convey.

As you use the book we pray that it will enable all people to declare, "We have a voice!"

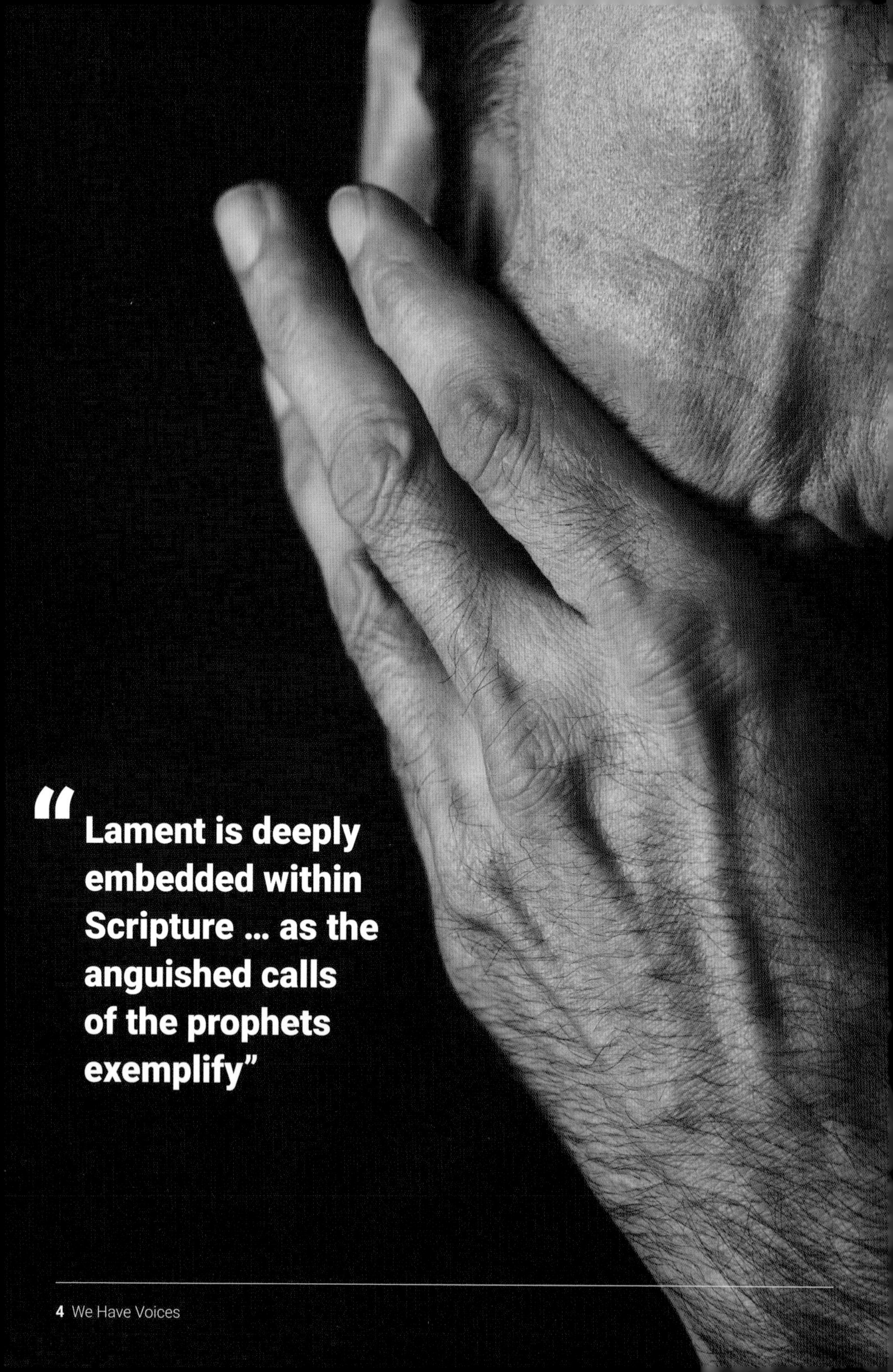

"Lament is deeply embedded within Scripture … as the anguished calls of the prophets exemplify"

Lament

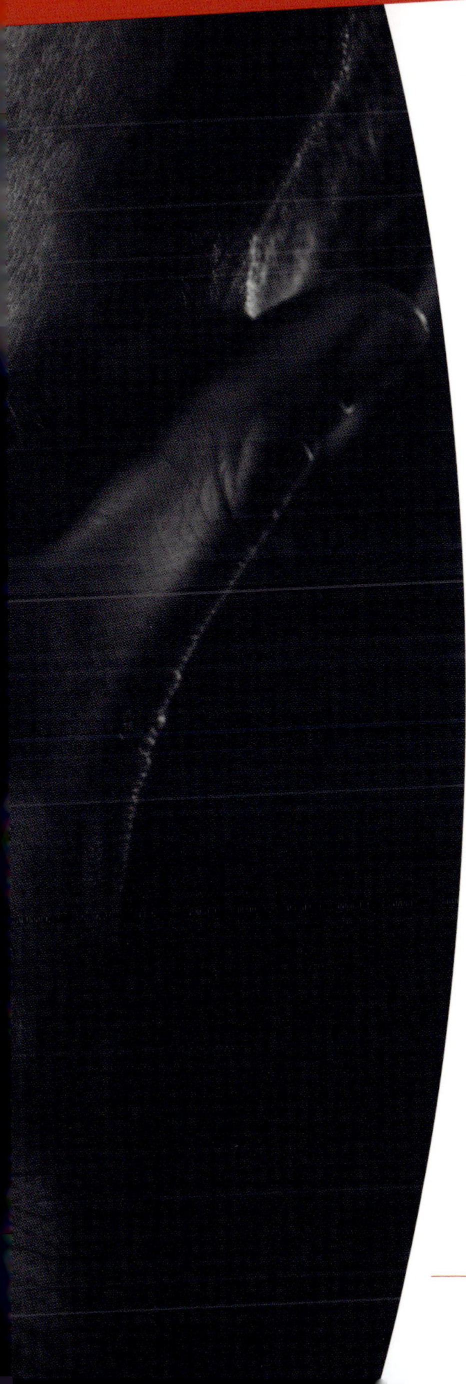

Most of us know how to moan or niggle, but a cry of frustration is not so often part of Sunday morning worship. However, the tradition of lament is deeply embedded within Scripture as the Psalms and the anguished calls of the prophets exemplify.

Maybe we have a tendency to 're-brand' this full-throated cry for justice as some polite prayers of confession from which we are swiftly absolved?

The following prayers and meditations are an invitation to hunker down with lament a little longer; to remind ourselves of the environmental and economic challenges that beset our beautiful and God-given world. They remind us of the divine intention that all people and the whole of creation should embody life in all abundance.

Guide us, Justice-seeking God,
for our vision is cloudy,
blinkered by our limited experience,
our ignorance and our bias.

Your thoughts are so much higher than ours,
your justice stretches beyond
our simple ideas of fairness,
your peace is so much deeper than the
removal of tension and conflict.

You call us to do justice in the midst of
our broken, messed-up world.
Teach us to love you with all our heart,
soul, mind and strength,
so that we can see clearly enough
what to do and how to act.
Give us grace to walk humbly with you,
acknowledging our weakness and frailty,
yet not fearing failure in our endeavour
to make a just world.
Guide us, impassion us, enable us.
For Jesus' sake.
Amen.

We speak of peace...
We long for justice...
We cry out for compassion...
And yet...

Our human stories are full of such seeking,
longing, and crying out,
from biblical epics to small town encounters,
from broken promises to disappointing
compromises.

If we could act with integrity for one hour,
not just the sponsored things
that serve ourselves more than others...

Or, if we could for just one moment
place ourselves in the shoes of people who suffer
so we might all have warm homes, security,
an education and employment...

Or, if we could stop and think before acting
in our own interests,
of the consequences to the earth, our
neighbours and ourselves...

If we could love each other as we love ourselves...
If we could only love as God loves us...
Unconditionally, inclusively, outrageously...
Then we could truly speak of peace, long for
justice and cry out for compassion.
We could be the change we seek
for our own sake, for our neighbour's sake,
for God's sake.
Amen.

Jesus, you so often greeted your disciples
with the words
"Do not be afraid."
With every fibre of my being I long to hear
those words from you,
"Do not be afraid."
Truth be told, I am afraid... no I'm not, I'm terrified!
There is so much war and hatred,
anger and violence,
it's really quite rational to be afraid.
You were no stranger to this and yet could still
eat with friends, weep with grief, and dance
with joy.
I pray for that peace which passes understanding
and eyes to see all that is indeed "very good"
in our harsh yet beautiful world.
May I learn to follow in your way
so that I too may speak the words of peace:
"Do not be afraid."
Amen.

Sovereign Lord,
In the beginning you tasked us to take care
of the earth and all that lives in it,
to work with you in your beautiful, fragile creation.
We grow more than enough food, raise more
than enough animals,
yet too many children's stomachs are
empty at night and as they go to school in
the morning.
Fields are turned to dust that blows away,
or are swept away by floods or destroyed
by storms we give quirky names.
Challenge us, your Church, your people,
to proclaim you as Sustainer of your
beautiful, fragile creation.
Amen.

A tree's prayer

To the One who holds the sun and rinses
out the clouds,
my ancestors told stories of you long before
I was a sapling,
you know my kind and my kind know you.
I thank you again for the fungi at my roots,
for the life-giving community you created beneath the
soil – that we might all survive and flourish and thrive
and know life in all its abundance.
I thank you for the birds that nest in my branches;
for the squirrels that run up my trunk; for the creepy
crawlies that are nourished on my leaves – the palms
of my hand held out offering sustenance to a world,
hardly seen, rarely noticed.
I miss them; I remember when these roots connected to a
woodland. I remember watching them felled for progress.
I miss them.
Today I see children playing in the park; dogs running
in the field; walkers rambling across the lace of mycelia
deep under foot.
I notice the little girl crying; the mum sat on her own; the dad
pushing children on swings. I see the teenagers discovering
their sense of self.
I will be around long after they have gone. I pray that
you will hold them close.
May they learn to do no damage to themselves or
the likes of me.
I hope they stand in fields and clap their hands, watching
the mountains bow down before you.
As they swing through the air and climb my branches, I hope
they get to know you as I know you: the Giver of Life.
Amen.

And Pilate said,
"What is truth?"
Wistful.
World-weary.
Administering 'justice'.
Maintaining 'peace'.
Washed his hands.
Wrote: "The King of the Jews".
The voice from the Cross:
"Father forgive them.
They know not what they do."
God stretches arms wide
for *all*.
Believe.
Amen.

God of justice and peace,
You call us to act justly, but our lives tell of how much our justice is rationed.
You call us to live in peace, but we are keen to keep machetes, guns and bombs by our side.
We have failed to admit our direct or indirect role in the way our world is tearing itself apart.
We have closed our ears to people's cries for justice and our eyes to faces that are hungry.

God of justice and peace,
Help us to pursue justice as if our very survival depends on it.
Help us to know that only a reconciled human race can prepare the way for your kingdom.
Forgive us for neglecting the urgency of your call for justice.
Forgive us for thinking we are immune to the consequences of war and injustice.
Help us to amend what we have been, and to live by the rules of your kingdom of peace and justice.
Amen.

We pray for your world:
exploited and exhausted by greed
and short-term gain;
earth left infertile;
waters poisoned;
habitat scorched and sea-levels rising.

Creator God, we fear for the future of your planet.
In your mercy, save us.

We pray for the human race:
divided and cruel, self-focused and uninformed;
children starving;
people violated or mutilated in battle;
people abused for their gender identity
or sexual orientation.

Saviour God, we fear for the future of your people.
In your mercy, save us.

We pray for ourselves:
broken, fragmented, lacking compassion;
unable to trust you and chained by guilt;
weak and ashamed, reluctant to love.

Spirit of God, we fear for the future of your Church.
In your mercy, save us.

In the name of the greatest gift, the Saviour
you sent us, Jesus Christ.
Amen.

He broke through the security.
Clambered on the table.
Screamed his lament:
"NO to FOSSIL FUEL!"
Scattered powder to mark his footprints.
Ruined the hallowed baize.
Was overcome and removed.

Stunned, some wept.
The mill wheels of LAW and ORDER
Began to grind.
The planet groaned:
"Oh GOD,
Where is JUSTICE?"

Somewhere the still, small voice breathes:
"Fear not, I AM."
Amen.

Generous God,
The wonders of your creation constantly astound us.
In the beginning, you declared it to be good.
A handful of earth contains more micro-organisms than there are people on the planet; soil and sea can provide sufficient to nourish all the people in the world; creation reflects the abundance of your provision for our needs. You instructed us to take care of it – yet we have betrayed the trust you gave us; we have been ignorant, greedy, clumsy and destructive.

We have not felt troubled that the essentials for our nourishment have been diminished to just a list of commodities on world markets, rather than being stewarded as our most vital resource.

We have not been concerned that farmers and growers worldwide frequently receive the lowest possible price for what they produce, in order to protect vested interests and profits.

We have not seen it as unjust that so many remain in poverty and hunger while others unashamedly indulge their appetites to excess.

We have not given time to source our food with skill and reverence, recognising it as sacramental.

Lord, forgive us.
Teach us to be thankful.
Teach us to be generous.
In the name of Jesus, the Bread of Life.
Amen.

Dear God,
We long for justice – for people to be freed from
the awfulness of oppression, victimisation, abuse,
marginalisation and enslavement. Yet, how can we
discern the path to justice?

Perhaps we can only find the path if we know the truth.
Unless we know the truth, there can be no justice.

We are bombarded with situations that cry out
for a just resolution,
in the mixture of fact and fiction bring us
towards the truth.
As we listen to stories, help us to find the deep
truth within them.
Amen.

God of our created world,
A globe in space full of a multitude of living things, from plants large and minute, to animals large and so small we cannot see them with a naked eye.
Everything has its place and inter-relates to enable a balance so that all can flourish within their setting and position in the food chains.
Yet the balance is distorted; the system out of sync; the creatures limited to less and less space; the oceans depleted.
Pollution and disregard for the natural world are rife.
Suffering of people is evident and increasing as the world warms.
The warnings of those who closely study the world's life and movements have been ignored and set aside.
Too little has been done to curb human greed.
We are thankful for the growing recognition that we must change our ways.
We ask for your help in learning to recognise when we have sufficient for our needs, and to live more simply, sharing gladly with people who have less.
Amen.

Creator God,
We confess that we have not been good caretakers of your creation.
We have treated this planet as a treasure to be exploited, rather than as a gift to be treasured;
we use the difficult and contradictory science as an excuse to do nothing;
we let the magnitude of the problem deter us.
Rather than seek forgiveness, we seek your help.
Help us to share rather than waste.
Help us to save rather than pollute.
Help us to be the stewards you appointed us to be.
Amen.

The following two prayers come from the Scotland District and Shetland District of the Methodist Church. They speak of particular situations that hold a mirror to our reactions to injustice.

She was introduced to me, Lord, after worship
one Sunday morning, in Partick, Glasgow.
You were there, Lord, you remember.
A war refugee.
Last Sunday, while out walking, she had
recognised a church building and chosen
to enter and joined in worship.
She was warmly welcomed.
She came back.
"Why does God allow war in Ukraine?"
were her first words.
She told me she lives in a cabin with her
15-year-old son, in a ship, moored in Braehead.
She showed me photographs on her mobile phone
of her cousins in camouflage, in trenches.
But it was the images of pet cats, left behind,
that brought tears.
I, having preached your word and led your people
in prayer, did not know what to say.
The weight of that question is much heavier when
it comes from such recent lived experience, such
live and ongoing violence.
Why, O Lord?
How long?
What on earth for, for heaven's sake?
Amen.

This virus came to us first known as a
respiratory disease,
restricting our capacity for breath,
requiring intervention that some might
keep on breathing.
O Breath of Life,
we wonder if we did enough,
if we had enough resources for timely action.
In justice and truth.
Lord, hear our prayer.

In Shetland, A4 posters in windows of shops and
churches and community halls and homes
declared "Shetland wi' Black Lives Matters".
This story came to us first known as a violent prejudice,
restricting one person's capacity for breath,
requiring intervention that some might keep
on breathing.
O sacred neck sore wounded,
we wonder if we do enough,
if we have enough resources for timely action.
In justice and truth.
Lord, hear our prayer.

And memories were stirred in Kirkcaldy,
Of Sheku and those charged to protect and serve,
And we wonder:
What happened?
How was it handled?
How was it investigated?
Was race a factor?
In justice and truth.
Lord, hear our prayer.
Amen.

Sheku Bayoh died on 3 May 2015 after an incident in the street in Kirkcaldy involving officers of Police Scotland. An independent public inquiry has been set up to examine the events surrounding the death.

Dear Holy God,
I am sorry I feel closest to you during my own
personal turmoil.
I reach out to you in fear and desperation over and over...
When I don't know where to turn, when all of my cards
have been played... there you still are: accepting my
tears, my pleas, my angst; all with quiet, loving,
all-knowing force. Protection.

I reach out to you in thanks and joy far too little. When little miracles make me smile; the notes people reach in songs that vibrate through my body; a line in a book that made me think. I appreciate them but the thanks don't leave my lips. You are still there, still loving, still all-knowing, but receiving nothing.

It takes my input to make this a two-way relationship.
To praise you, not just need you.
I need to understand where I've been to know where I am now. You have seen and understood it all.
My past, my present, my future.

I even questioned writing this. How was I worthy?
And there you were: whispering phrases, helping me see things, hear things, write things.

I hope to know you more. I know you know me already.
Amen.

Oh Jerusalem, Jerusalem, beloved city,
how we long for peace and justice to walk in your streets and markets,
for peace and equity to join hands!
Your heart is broken and your people shattered.
How long, oh God, before your people are sheltered in safety under the shadow of your wings?
Show us how to live as neighbours, side by side and face to face.
Bring us to our senses.
Teach us that the language of hatred only escalates violence and war is never a solution for division.
How long before we hear your voice, spoken through the ages?
How long until we learn the lessons of love?
How long before justice and mercy flow like an everlasting stream?
Amen.

“...to intercede for others requires us to stand in solidarity with them”

Solidarity

Prayers of intercession can often sound like a shopping list of impossible wishes that, once said, require no further response. But to intercede for others requires us to stand in solidarity with them – to put our bodies where our beliefs are – and to go from worship to make tangible changes in our communities.

We often tell ourselves that our churches have few resources and our power to effect change is very limited, yet if we look around at what can be achieved in small ways by people whom others may think powerless then we should be encouraged.

The following prayers and meditations name a number of issues and particular places; there will be others that you will want to add from the headlines or your personal experience. These prayers of solidarity remind us of our collective and international responsibilities to strive for justice for the very poorest people of the world. This is not wishful thinking but our calling.

God of peace and justice,
Help us to listen carefully
and learn from people who have been made to
walk the path of injustice.
Help us to hear well
and to hold with gentleness and respect people in pain.
Help us to see clearly
and grasp where truth has been distorted to preserve
the privilege of some.
Help us know truly
and to understand the effects of relentless
discrimination, dismissal and rejection.
Helps us to act faithfully
in ways that do not rob any one of us of our agency,
but by standing alongside each other in our
search for justice.
Help us to persevere
and not to settle for superficial solutions
to complex problems,
or to act in ways that allow us to feel better
but bring no new life and liberty to people
unjustly treated.
Rather, help us to face the truth of ourselves
and the world,
with resurrection hope, making all things new.
Most of all loving God, help us be open to your grace,
to build communities of harmony where all of
us are welcome,
all of us are safe,
all of us can flourish,
and where the bonds between people, communities,
nations, generations,
and all living things are enhanced.
Amen.

We do not ask for strength, we have strength;
we pray for resolve to use our strength for good.

We do not ask for courage, we have courage;
we pray for resilience to rise above defeats.

We do not ask for acceptance, we are acceptable;
we pray for persistence to demand equality for all.

We do not ask for a voice, we have voices;
we pray for determination to speak love's
truth to power.

As Susannah Wesley used her insight, learning and strength to educate her children equally, we pray that we, indeed all people, will continually use our wisdom, courage and diversity to turn the tables on injustice and embrace equity for all.
Amen.

For those of us hiding from destructive
actions of aggressors,
for those of us in fear of forced personal intimacy,
for those of us unable to find sufficient food as crops fail,
for those of us exploited as we seek safety,
for those of us forced to return to dangerous situations,
for those of us who have never seen an ocean, but risk
life in overcrowded dinghies,
for those of us arriving in new places,
may each of us sense the closeness of your Spirit giving
strength and courage for each moment of our days.
May your presence guide us to safety; to a place where
life is secure and skills utilised.
Amen.

Creator of life and giver of light,
We pray for situations where your light is
shrouded in darkness:

For places of war and oppression;
for children terrorised, families scattered,
their lives unravelling and falling apart;
for the ongoing nightmare of torture and rape.

Help us to know that your light is woven
into the fabric of our world
and to trust in your sustaining love.

We pray for refugees fleeing their homes,
cast adrift on seas of fear and desperation;
for those living in the land of the lost
who stand alone, unseen and unmet in
life's struggles.

We hold before you those situations where
your light is shrouded in darkness
and we remember all people who need your
light and love.

Silence

Creator of life, in your name we pray.
Amen.

God of justice,
We pray for all people the world considers to be at the 'bottom of the pile':
for people who have no status or wealth or influence,
for people who are disregarded.
Forgive us for actions that have led to the dehumanisation of others.
We pray for people who are oppressed, people in poverty, people with disabilities, people whose belief or way of living is different from ours.
We pray for people who are bought and sold and treated like commodities, held as slaves and forced to work for others whose only interest is the profit they will make.
Forgive us for making selfish consumer choices when some have no choices.
Forgive our apathy towards modern slavery, lead us into action and change.
We seek your justice for a world in need of you, not just for our smaller world in which we exist and operate, but for a whole world, where life is to be lived in peace and justice to its most full, and each person is released to realise their full potential.
We commit to be people of justice for the sake others, in Jesus' name.
Amen.

We thank you God for people who parent
on their own.
We remember prayerfully all those who either
by deliberate decision
or despite death, divorce, desertion or disaster,
remain strong and committed to the children
whom they raise alone.
We thank God that we can see a commitment
to parenting which mirrors the love of
the parent God to Jesus, the beloved Son.
If people who parent alone are blamed for
troublesome children or family breakdown,
let us be mindful of their stubborn resilience
in the face of prejudicial assumptions.
Jesus, whose mother remained faithful to her
child, even to death,
we thank you, for the faithful witness of people
who parent on their own.
Amen.

Jesus, who fed five thousand with food to spare,
I did not choose to have an empty larder.
It is not my fault that my children are hungry.
I have to put on a brave face to go to the foodbank,
I have consistently swallowed my pride.
I do not wish to live by another's benevolence,
like I owe someone a favour, because putting stuff in the box makes a stranger feel better about their full supermarket trolley.
I don't have enough, because many have too much:
second homes, food left over, more and more 'stuff'.
I don't want pity, I want justice.
I don't want crumbs, I want to sit at the table.
I am not underserving poor, I am beautiful, made in God's image.
I deserve the whole menu of my rights.
Amen.

(Based on words of Bishop Desmond Tutu)

Lord of change and transformation,
Through your love for us, you transform our hearts and minds. Through your presence in us, you transform our lives. We praise you for that and thank you for pouring out your love and grace. As your followers, you call us to respond to that grace. You challenge us to be people of transformation in this broken world. You want us to be your hands and feet on earth. You want us to show love, care, and compassion for others, just like you did. You call us to be change-makers in this unjust world. When that task seems too big Lord, equip us. Let your Spirit use us and guide us.

Lord of change and transformation,
We pray for organisations that tackle inequality and stand up for justice. We pray particularly for foodbanks and similar organisations.
Thank you for all the provisions that keep this work going; the generous donations from people and places. Bless each person who gives and each person who receives. Bring hope and comfort to those that need it.
Thank you for all the staff, volunteers and guests. Give them wisdom when they need it and shine through them as they show compassion and empathy.
Lord, shine your light in the hearts of politicians and decision makers. Use your people and your power to bring changes to this country. Bring an end to poverty and an end to economic injustice.
We offer our prayers to you now.
Amen.

"Give us this day our daily bread" – if only life were so simple...
If only I didn't have to be confronted by such a bewilderingly wide product choice, special promotions, price comparisons, told to 'buy one, get one free'.
Was it Gandhi who said "Live simply that others may simply live"? Was it easier then than it is now?

Lord, my shopping habits make me complicit in many of the practices of which I claim to disapprove. My shopping experience means I take for granted the variety, quantity and quality of the food which I buy. Phrases like 'sustainability', 'ethical sourcing', 'carbon footprint', become just theoretical concepts, unrelated to real life, real shopping. The connections, physical, economic and human, between field and kitchen remain vague in my mind.

God, as I make my food choices, awaken in me the need to respect and love the beautiful planet you have made. Make me willing to be inconvenienced if necessary. Make me willing to pay a fair price for a fair product. Disrupt the plans of those who sell inferior and unhealthy products under the guise of 'money saving', and may sufficient good food be accessible and affordable to all.

In the name of Jesus, who did not hesitate to disrupt unfair trade in the Temple.
Amen.

To know the love of Christ
that surpasses knowledge
so that we may be filled
with the fullness of God.
(Ephesians 3:19, NRSV)

That is our desire, Lord,
but do we desire it enough for others?
Enough not only to cry out to you
for things to be different,
but enough to cry out
to those who can make a difference,
for things to be different.
The arc of your story
is your especial love for
the widow, orphan and stranger,
sending your righteous prophets
to challenge powerful kings,
and ultimately sending your Son.
May we be so filled with the love of Christ
that we will do our uttermost to bring fullness
of life to others.
Amen.

If we have used the word 'blind' to signify
narrow mindedness...
If we have used the word 'deaf' to mean
wilful disregard...
If we have used the word 'lame' to imply weakness...
If we have used the word 'dumb' as a synonym
for stupid...
If we have used the word 'mad' to pigeonhole
ideas that contradict our own...
then transform our language, re-form our words
so that we who are blind might see most clearly,
and we who are deaf hear different songs,
we who are lame may dance in stillness
and we who are dumb have wisdom beyond speech,
we who are mad might have secret insight
and we who are nowhere near perfect,
be the hopeful presence
within this beautiful yet broken world.
Amen.

God of all creation,
Like the flowers of the field, we are all different colours. We thank you.
We thank you, holy God.

Like the fish in the sea, we are all different sizes. We thank you.
We thank you, holy God.

Creator God, you made us all wonderfully and beautifully, with our own abilities, looks and thought processes. We thank you.
We thank you, holy God.

Peaceful God, we marvel at how you ensured all your creation lives in harmony, but are ashamed of when we do not live in harmony with our siblings in Christ. Please teach us this skill to accept others for who they are. We thank you.
We thank you, holy God.

Inclusionary God, we thank you for the balance of your creation, where creatures, trees and insects live together in the same space, but we are appalled that we have not done the same for our fellow siblings. Please teach us to fling our doors wide and be a Church of the world. We thank you.
We thank you, holy God.

This is our prayer now and every day, and we thank you.
We thank you, holy God.
Amen.

God of justice,
You long for everyone to have life in all its fullness;
help us to refuse to accept inequality and poverty.
You yearn for a right relationship with people and planet;
help us to enable a flourishing of all creation.
You created one people and one world;
help us to stand for justice for all people seeking refuge.
You fashioned everyone in your own image;
help us to resist all forms of discrimination.
You desire justice and reconciliation for all people
and nations;
help us to be peace-builders in our lives and in the world.
May your justice roll like a mighty river,
your righteousness like an ever-flowing stream.
And may your people say,
Amen.

God of peace and reconciliation,
We pray for people who suffer as a result of war
and armed conflict.

We hold before you people who are victims of our inhumanity
towards each other.
Remembering especially children whose lives have
been damaged:
Children who have witnessed horrors, who were abused,
who had to flee as refugees and who have been forced
to fight as child soldiers.
For all innocent people who bear seen and unseen wounds,
we pray for healing, justice, hope and peace.

We pray for people who carry wounds in body, mind and spirit
as a result of taking an active part in war:
For the military veterans who answered the call to fight and
now battle with torments and horrors as a consequence of
their role in combat.
Be with them in the dark hours of night when the raging
demons of guilt, shame and mental trauma attack. Help them
as they struggle to be reconciled to the things they saw, did or
were unable to do on the battlefield.
For all broken people who bear seen and unseen wounds,
we pray for healing, justice, hope and peace.

God who loves all people, help us to overcome our prejudices
to seek true justice, peace and reconciliation for all who carry
the scars of conflict, whether they are the victims or the
perpetrators of violence.
For all of us who struggle to forgive, who bear wounds, who
suffer the long-term effects of trauma, seen and unseen,
we pray for healing, justice, hope and peace.
Amen.

Creator God,
You formed us from the dust of the earth,
breathing into us precious life, uniqueness and divine purpose.
Wipe away the stain of hate and prejudice,
so that we may see afresh your image reflected in all people,
beyond our ceaseless desire to label and divide.

Fill our hearts with renewed purpose to safeguard the vulnerable,
and whenever the voice of justice is silenced through fear or indifference,
inspire in us a tenacity to challenge injustice
and a determination to seek urgent change.

We ask this in the name of your loving Son,
our Saviour, Jesus Christ.
Amen.

And how will justice flow or righteousness
stream like a mighty torrent?
Only when in the tears of those who,
even while oppressed,
have vision enough to hold fast;
Only, even while the oceans swallow
up the fugitives,
people hold out compassionate arms of rescue;
Only when those, still blooded by regimes
of suppression,
mount protest for freedom and human dignity;
Only, even when the rains continue to flood the
parchment of land,
there are those writing treatise of environmental
equality in their actions and on their hearts.
Justice will flow only when, despite the gullies of
tears and deluge of blood,
the sacrificial compassion and action of the brave
dam the inrush of destruction.
Justice will only flow
when human love showers into the landscape
of inequalities
in which we are all nomads.
Then justice will roll down as a river,
and righteousness as a mighty stream;
Only then will judgment flow down like water,
and righteousness as an impassable torrent.
Amen.

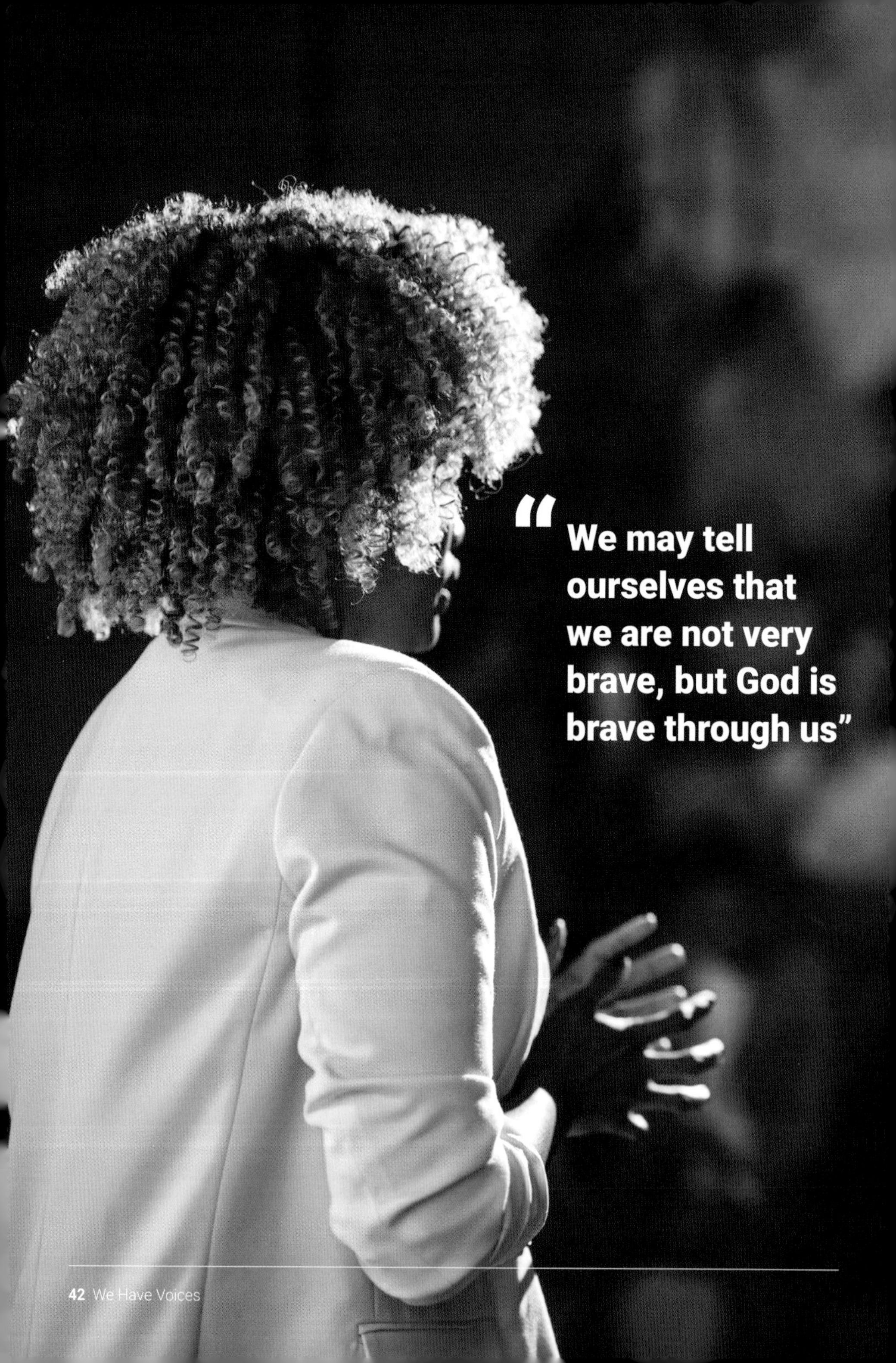

> **"We may tell ourselves that we are not very brave, but God is brave through us"**

Courage

To commit ourselves as Christian communities to follow the justice-seeking God is an act of courageous commitment. Following Jesus requires us to open our hearts and minds to the suffering of others and to make sacrificial choices in order to enact transformational change. We may tell ourselves that we are not very brave, but God is brave through us, and if we are able to take a step towards the kingdom, we will find that Jesus will fall into step beside us.

In these prayers and meditations we hear how the voice of lament can be called into action, how we can open our eyes to inequalities and begin to change the balance of power.

Jesus was very clear that following him is not an easy path, we are called to risk everything for love.

God who is justice,
Maybe we cannot find what we search for
until we open our hands in exasperation,
in anticipation,
in submission,
until we let go of our striving for justice
as a concept
and realise it is in our hands to craft
a better, more equitable world.
Amen.

Our living God,
We give thanks that your love is matched
by your commitment to justice.

May we, by the power of the Holy Spirit,
be inspired to stand up for truth and justice,
and against any behaviours and attitudes that
do not reflect Christ's values.

Give us a heart that desires to stand alongside
people pushed to the margins
by a society that prefers to judge the external,
rather than examine the contents of the heart.

Lord, enable us to offer the hope found in Christ,
to those who only know despair.
And may we always be agents of peace
and harmony,
in a world that prefers to study war and
foment discord.

And we pray for greater signs of your kingdom
coming among us,
and ask that these may be manifested in us.

This we ask in Jesus' name,
Amen.

God of justice,
We thank you that justice is both your gift
and our calling.
Forgive us when we forget and think it is someone else's responsibility.
Forgive us when we fear that seeking justice will cost us our comfort.
Forgive us when we hope that the issues will go away without us getting involved.
We pray especially for people broken by systems built on injustice.
Let their cry be not unheard, let their pain not be ignored, let their voices be clear.
Help us to stand alongside each other, to listen with care and to act in unison so that justice may come.
God, in your mercy
hear our prayer.

God of power,
We thank you that power is the strength
to achieve good.
Forgive us when we think we are powerless, believing we can change nothing and disregarding the gifts we are given.
Forgive us when we misuse the power we have for our own ends and not for the common good.
We pray for people in positions of great influence and power;
leaders of nations, politicians, writers, celebrities and media influencers,
that all may have the wisdom to use power to enable all to flourish.
God, in your mercy
hear our prayer.

God of truth,
Give us the courage to face the reality of the world
we have created and damaged,
in which our attitudes and actions have added to
already heavy burdens.
We especially pray for this extraordinary planet and
its many life forms.
We confess that what human beings have done
has destroyed beauty, disrupted harmony and
threatened creatures with extinction.
Help us to lament, repent and work for restoration
and renewal.
God, in your mercy
hear our prayer.

Gracious God,
Give us a vision of our world as your love
would make it:
a world where the weak are protected, and
none go hungry or live in poverty;
a world where the riches of life are shared by all;
a world where different races, nations and cultures
can live together in joy;
a world where peace is built with justice, and justice
is guided by love;
and give us the inspiration and courage to build it,
through Jesus Christ our Lord.
Amen.

Great Spirit,
Let your ravaged sequoia and toxic oceans
confront us;
let the oil-choked cormorant and charred
koala compel us;
silencing our pointless and distracting chatter
and calling us to account because
as a species we seem too dim to make
good choices.
Let our hearts be troubled.
Let our ways be disrupted.
Let our souls reconnect with you, with life,
through the mediation of your other creatures
who have suffered us too long.
Save us from our destructive arrogance,
our willful self-deceptions,
and the ignorance of unintended consequences.
Disarm us, disempower us,
until we learn to grieve, and to hear your voice as
the cry of the eagle and song of the whale and
the joyful clapping of the trees of the fields.
Amen.

Loving and generous God,
In a world of inequality, war and destruction,
we often find ourselves conflicted.
Guide us to follow your way, and let us hear your encouragement to swim against the current,
Lord, strengthen us.

When we feel the need to conform where we should bring challenge, and when we feel more comfortable in the company of power than at the margins, Lord, wake us.

When we separate the poor into deserving and undeserving, and when we support others for our own gain, Lord, help us.

When we count our blessings ostentatiously and praise you loudly to make us look better and more valued than others, Lord, remind us of who will be the last.

When we try to justify our privilege, share only our surplus and explain away your call to radical justice, Lord, forgive us.

In you, justice-seeking God, is always
a new beginning.
If we want to change, you invite us to start afresh.
Lord, be with us as we follow Christ's example: may we be gentle peacemakers, non-violent protesters, and confident challengers.
May we be those who live out your kingdom values and inspire others to follow the journey.
May your kingdom come and your will be done.
Amen.

God of all people and all generations,
We raise a joyful song to you, because you are good, and your love endures forever! You mercifully touch the untouchable leper in love and with healing, but you also overturn tables in anger at injustice.

In our weakness, empower us to challenge unjust powers that oppress. Equally, O Christ, enable us to show and speak love and mercy where necessary. Help us always to get the balance right – to speak truth to power, but also to show grace and to speak your life-giving word where it is needed.

Liberator God, free us from evil systems, mindsets, activities and structures that falsely and positively express themselves in our personal, collective and institutional life as the need for belonging, identity and expression of difference. Energise us to work for and prepare for a moment in time, a place and a way of living together, where we see Christ in each other and reflect Christ to one another.

Our hope is in your unfailing love, O Great Shield. Shelter us and watch over us, O Great Protector. But, help us not to be a hidden people, O Great Energy Giver. Paint our hearts with brushes of your love and compassion. Inspire and enable us to find new ways to be a force of love and justice, a witness for you during these times.
Amen.

God of all, who brought creation into being and continues to weave and make, create and inspire, we come to you aware of discrimination, bias, injustice and prejudice in our world, communities, fellowships and selves; awake to the all-encompassing love you have for your children, its vastness, diversity and intricacies.
God of all, we commit ourselves to prayer and action, with open hearts and minds.

Living God, in our encounters through life with people, places and organisations, may we recognise discrimination and injustice and become better listeners and learners. Open our hearts and minds to new understandings and appreciations of how life and faith are experienced by others.
Living Lord, we commit ourselves to listening and learning to others and you.

Living God, as we engage with controversy and awkward conversations, may we always remember that all are made in your image, precious in your sight, worthy of your love. May your love for all be our inspiration as we are challenged, changed and comforted by your call for justice.
Living Lord, we commit ourselves to being challenged, changed and comforted by others and you.

Living God, equip us with energy, compassion and wisdom
as we challenge the realities of prejudice and injustice
in our communities and fellowships. May we strive to
be equipped by your Holy Spirit as we stand alongside,
support and love our neighbours wholeheartedly.
Living Lord, we commit ourselves to being allies
against prejudice in your name.
Amen.

Holy God,
We learn that you are great and glorious,
King of Kings and Lord of Lords.
Scripture tells of your grandeur and majesty.

And yet...
...you are also the God of looking closely.

You are the God in the still and the small.
You are the God of noticing sparrows and
numbering the hairs on a human head.
You are the God constrained in human flesh,
in touch with your world.
We learn that you have an eye for the little things.

Take my little things, Lord:
my daft joy at the seed that grows
and delight in the shiny beetle on the path;
my confused attempts to get the recycling right
and understand my carbon footprint;
my noticing of neighbour and stranger with small acts
of kindness.

Take my one small life and make it part of something bigger:
a tide of justice and goodness sweeping through your world,
challenging the mighty in their seats of power,
disrupting the forces of destruction, apathy and evil
with the force of ridiculous love.

Take my life into yours, and yours into mine.
And make even my little life a part of your
great work of loving and redeeming your world.
Amen.

With thankful hearts, we look and see the richness of our lives.
With sorrowful hearts, we confess that our wealth can make us overlook the needs of others.
With thankful hearts, we recall how other people add to our lives.
With sorrowful hearts, we confess that we have benefited from the undervaluing of others.
With thankful hearts, we enjoy the simple pleasures of human fellowship.
With sorrowful hearts, we confess our disproportionate value on material possessions.
With thankful hearts, we explore all that is new and different.
With sorrowful hearts, we confess that we limit our own horizons to the people and ideas that are familiar.

Father, let our thanksgiving open our eyes and not close them,
let our thanksgiving draw our gaze up and beyond,
let our thanksgiving reveal what we need to hold on to and what we need to let go.
Amen.

Dear Father Mother God,
Creator and Sustainer,
your generous provision is for all.
Songs of thanks and praise rise worldwide.

But, selfish greed and lust for power
wither our love with ingratitude.

Forgive us, Father Mother.
We are sorry.
It is impossible to make amends!
Help us, please.

Mercy overcomes injustice.
The cost borne on the Cross.
Christ's compassion is peace.

As you call us, so we come:
'Come as a little child, trusting,
and follow me'.
Amen.

The following prayer was written to remember the many ethnic groups living under military rule in Myanmar since 2021. It has been adapted so that it can be used to remind us of the many parts of the world where people live under oppressive regimes, but we hope that you will also keep in your prayers the people of Myanmar.

We pray that all who live in countries where ethnic groups seek to maintain their unique identities, embrace each other and live together in unity – just as diverse species of plants shine their glory in a garden. We pray for people across the world who live under military rule, for hope and peace in a time of uncertainty; for the quest for the restoration of democratic government; for political activists and prisoners; and for civilian victims of civil war. We pray for internally displaced people and refugees in neighbouring countries. We are mindful of humanitarian organisations that work with people in need, poverty-stricken communities and children and young people in conflict areas – especially working for their education. We remember those who teach in government schools, colleges and churches and for all who maintain justice for others in hospitals, community schools and evangelistic work amidst the political crises.
Amen.

Jesucristo, Señor del tiempo, de la vida y de la historia,
Acudimos a ti desde la enfermedad y el sufrimiento de nuestros pueblos.
En tu palabra de vida encontramos
esperanza para este mundo desesperanzado,
y encontramos caminos de justicia, alegría y paz.

Jesucristo, Señor del tiempo, de la vida y de la historia,
Danos del agua de vida, que cura y sana tanta enfermedad,
egoísmo y exclusión.

Jesucristo, Señor del tiempo, de la vida y la historia,
Ayúdanos a vivir en compromiso mutuo con todos
los que nos rodean,
a defendiendo y cuidando la vida, especialmente
de los más desprotegidos,
afirmándonos como comunidades de esperanza,
consuelo, y aliento.

Jesucristo, Señor del tiempo, de la vida y de la historia,
Clamamos por la sanación y restauración de la casa
común que nos diste,
en la seguridad de que otro cielo y otra tierra son posibles.

Jesucristo, Señor del tiempo, de la vida y de la historia,
Desde tu gracia amorosa afirmamos que tu proyecto
para la humanidad nunca fue un proyecto de destrucción,
sino promesa de vida abundante.

Página siguiente

Jesus Christ, Lord of time, of life and of history,
We come to you from the sickness and suffering
of our peoples.
In your word of life may we find hope for this hopeless world,
and ways of justice, joy and peace.

Jesus Christ, Lord of time, of life and of history,
Give us the water of life, which heals and cures so much
sickness, selfishness and exclusion.

Jesus Christ, Lord of time, life and history,
Help us to commit to live in harmony with all
those around us,
to protect and care for one another, especially
for the most vulnerable,
affirming us as communities of hope, comfort,
and encouragement.

Jesus Christ, Lord of time, of life and of history,
We cry out for the healing and restoration of the shared
home you gave us,
in the assurance that another heaven and another
earth are possible.

Jesus Christ, Lord of time, of life and of history,
Out of your loving grace we affirm that your plan
for humanity was never a project of destruction,
but a promise of abundant life.

Continued overleaf

Jesucristo, Señor del tiempo, de la vida y de la historia,
Afirmamos que tu voluntad no es ni el dolor, ni la enfermedad, ni la muerte.
Ninguno de los males que padece este mundo son tu voluntad, sino que son parte de nuestro pecado.

Jesucristo, Señor del tiempo, de la vida y de la historia,
Te pedimos la fuerza, el coraje y la voluntad
para ser hacedores del bien en el día malo.
Conduce y fortalece a tu iglesia y a todas sus comunidades
para ser señales y signos, aunque pequeñas,
de esperanza y vida buena.
Amén.

Jesus Christ, Lord of time, of life and of history,
We affirm that your will is neither pain, nor
sickness, nor death.
None of the evils from which this world suffers
are your will, but are part of our sin.

Jesus Christ, Lord of time, of life and of history,
We ask you for the strength, the courage and the will to do
good in the midst of evil.
Lead and strengthen your church and all its communities
to be signs and symbols, however small,
of hope and a good life.
Amen.

Sometimes it is hard to be part of this world.
We see the ugliness of violence, and the consequence of hatred.
We see the cycle of vengeance, and the justification of prejudice.

But we worship a God who loved this world so much.
As Jesus he chose to be part of it,
he was hurt by its violence and condemned by its hatred.
Yet God loves it still, weeps with it, works with it, saves it and redeems it.

As God's people, let us choose to be part of God's world
as we witness to the redeeming power of costly love.
Amen.

Prince of Peace,
We pray for peace for those nations where there is war and conflict.
We pray that war-mongers would have a change of heart.
In a world of violence, we long for the day when swords are beaten into ploughshares and learn war no more.
We give thanks for the peace-builders and reconcilers of the past.
We pray for those who now stand in the gap between oppressor and oppressed in the hope of bringing reconciliation,
where there are no winners and losers but a new wholeness.
Prince of Peace, hear our prayer.
Amen.

O Dduw, dywed dy air wrthym ein bod fel un teulu sy'n perthyn i'r Meseia Iesu. Iesu yw'r un sy'n ein galw ni atat ti ac at ein gilydd fel brodyr a chwiorydd. Diolch i ti am yr holl bethau da rwyt wedi eu haddo i bob un ohonom yn Iesu, a diolch nad yw'r rhain yn ddibynnol ar bwy ydym o ran ein cefndir, oed, hil, iaith, lliw ein croen, rhywedd neu abledd neu statws. Fe'n gwnaed pob un ar dy lun a'th ddelw di i dderbyn bywyd yn ei holl gyflawnder ac i fod yn un yng Nghrist. Diolch, Arglwydd.

Cyffeswn ein bod yn syrthio'n brin o'r hyn a fwriadwyd i ni fod oherwydd nad ydym weithiau yn deall, neu'n cydnabod neu'n cofleidio dy ewyllys. Weithiau byddwn yn anghofio pwy ydym ni ynot ti, a byddwn mor aml yn methu gweld pobl eraill fel yr wyt ti'n eu gweld nhw. Mae'n ddrwg gennym am golli cyfleoedd i sefyll dros hawliau eraill, i gynnig cymorth mewn adfyd, i geisio cymod a heddwch. Maddau i ni, Dad.

Gan gydnabod ein bod ni'n rhan o dy gynllun di i wireddu dy ddyhead ar gyfer holl bobl y byd, ymrwymwn ein hunain yn awr i geisio bywyd yn ei holl gyflawnder i bawb, i ymateb i'r anghenion a welwn yn ein byd, ac i geisio cyfiawnder a heddwch ym mhob amgylchiad, trwy gymorth dy Ysbryd Glân. Clyw ein gweddi yn enw Iesu.
Amen.

(Yn seiliedig ar Galatiaid 3:26-29)

O God, your word tells us that we are like one family who belong to the Messiah, Jesus. Jesus is the one who calls us to you and to each other as brothers and sisters. Thank you for all the blessings you have promised to all of us in Jesus, and thank you that these are not dependent on who we are in terms of our background, age, race, language, skin colour, gender, ability or status. We were all made in your image and likeness to receive life in all its fullness and to be one in Christ. Thank you, Lord.

We confess that we fall short of what we could be because we sometimes do not understand, recognise or embrace your will. Sometimes we forget who we are in you, and we so often fail to see other people as you see them. We are sorry for missing opportunities to stand up for the rights of others, to offer help in adversity, to seek reconciliation and peace. Forgive us, Father.

Recognising that we are part of your plan to realise your desire for all the people of the world, we commit ourselves now to seek life in all its fullness for everyone, to respond to the needs we see in our world, and to seek justice and peace in all circumstances, through the help of your Holy Spirit. Hear our prayer in the name of Jesus.
Amen.

(Based on Galatians 3:26-29)

We pray for peace in this world today. Each day we see stories of war, struggle and suffering and we pray for your peace over this world. We pray that people will know your love and blessing over their lives, that your peace may enter into situations where there seems to be none.

We pray for the ending of all conflict in the name of religion. We pray that harmony and love would be present and your voice of peace would bring calm to conversations and arguments.

We pray for world leaders at this time. We pray that their actions may not be for their own growth and power but with the intention of making this world a better, more peaceful place. We pray that your hand will be over each decision made by these leaders, directing them to where there is greatest need and aiding in the development of peace.

We pray for war-torn countries and people who live under constant pressure of war at this time. We pray for peace for the population in these countries, that they know safety and peace over their families. We pray for people who are called up without choice, that they might know your presence in the field and be guided by you in their actions.

We pray for persecuted groups in the world; people who cannot feel safe or feel that they are unable to be who they truly are where they live. We pray that governments and legislators in these countries will see what they are doing as forms of persecution and seek to enact peace and reconciliation with those who are hurting due to the situation they find themselves in.

Amen.

This prayer was written for Stephen Lawrence Day. Stephen Lawrence was murdered in a racially-motivated attack at the age of 18 when studying for his A levels. He was dreaming of becoming an architect. The subsequent police investigation was controversially flawed and Stephen Lawrence's family's tireless campaign for justice brought a change to the double jeopardy laws and also resulted in the establishment of Racial Justice Sunday.

Liberating Spirit of God,
We pray Lord, have mercy on us,
forgive us for our prejudices,
forgive us for our complacency,
forgive us for our assumed supremacy,
forgive us for our insensitivity to the racial discrimination in the world,
forgive us for being narrow in our vision of the world around us,
forgive us for being untouched by the injustice of racism happening in our world,
forgive us for being silent spectators to racial attacks on our sisters and brothers,
forgive us for compromising our Christian discipleship which affirms racial justice,
forgive us for normalising oppressive status quos and for the division of 'us' and 'them'.

Empowering Spirit of God,
We pray for the pedagogy of the oppressed,
help our education systems to provide fair,
inclusive, safe spaces for young people.

We pray for our dreams for a just world,
help us to dream and strive for a world where
equality, peace, love and justice will thrive.
We pray for the public institutions, civil society,
faith communities and for churches,
help us to affirm transparency and accountability
for justice in all cases and at all times.
Help us to realise that injustice anywhere is a threat
to justice everywhere.

We pray for advocacy and campaigns for justice
for our creation,
help us as faith communities to be prophets
of justice, to be forerunners of inclusion, to
be champions of love, to be practitioners of
compassion and to be channels of life in
all its fullness.
May your courage lead us and strengthen us
in this, our commitment for peace and justice.
Amen.

Loving God,
Your justice flows like a river and your righteousness like a never-ending stream,
we re-commit ourselves today to being your Church, seeking your justice on earth.

Where injustice causes unfathomable pain and suffering,
we seek your deep ocean of love and peace.
Give us humility and compassion to nurture relationships that restore justice.

Where there are overwhelming and unyielding injustices,
we seek your powerful torrent of water to wear them away.
Give us bravery and persistence to break apart the causes of injustice.

At times when the ground seems parched and injustice is everywhere,
we seek your underground streams of resistance and renewal.
Give us faithfulness and endurance to uncover life-giving waters of justice.

When we look for refuge in complaint and complacency and easy answers,
we seek to journey upstream together in search of your justice,
flowing freely to all, transforming people, bringing peace and renewing creation.
Through Christ we pray.
Amen.

God, who in Jesus fled as a refugee straight
from the manger,
Grant us your compassion to welcome the stranger,
and offer sanctuary to people fleeing from danger.

God, as Immanuel who promised to never
leave us alone,
challenge us as a Church to never leave people
to walk alone,
but to provide friendship, shelter, food, and
show love.

God, the Spirit who speaks the many languages
of the migrants,
may we celebrate multi-cultural ethnic diversity
as our nation's vibrancy,
striving together for peace, love and justice
as our community's reliance.

God, who is united as three in one in blessed Trinity,
make us known to one another, so that we do not
walk alone, loving and gracious God.
Amen.

God of a thousand hills,
help us resist litanies of scarcity.
You have given us life in abundance,
let us not tell ourselves there is not enough
for everyone.

God of the mirrored lakes,
help us to resist litanies of helplessness.
You have given us power to change the world,
let us not tell ourselves changes are beyond
our control.

God of the tea plantations,
help us to resist litanies of individualistic capitalism.
You have given us eyes to see and generous hearts,
let us not tell ourselves we are paralysed by
economic forces.

God of the rain forest,
help us to resist litanies of apocalyptic
climate change.
You have offered us redemption from
our greedy lives,
let us not tell ourselves responsibility
lies beyond us.

God of the rice paddy,
help us to resist litanies of deprivation.
You have provided us with fertile soil and
water in due season,
let us not tell ourselves we have a right to eat when
others are hungry.

God of the sunrise,
help us resist litanies of hopelessness.
You have promised fullness of life to all,
let us live humbly and live lives of mercy
and justice.
Amen.

“We are called to be activists for justice and protagonists of peace”

Sending

The blessing we receive at the end of a service is not a passive thing, it is a sending out, a call to enter the place of worship that is the world, the workplace, the community and the public square. Our public worship reminds us of the liturgies of everyday life to which we need to be alert during the week. Ordinary existence has a liturgical shape. We can lament over the morning news or be inspired to action as we walk to work. Repentance and blessing are around us all the time; and wherever and whenever we worship, we are recalled to be mindful of our place within creation and our responsibilities across the world.

We are called to be activists for justice and protagonists of peace. These prayers draw together the voice of lament, commitment and courage and send us out into the world in the power of the Spirit to be the lived reality of our spoken faith. Here, we are given not only a personal reassurance of God's abiding love, but a challenge to bring that reassurance to others, in practical everyday ways.

Summer
Who knew you painted with
so many shades of green?
Who knew so many other plants and critters
would long for my earthy treasures?
Now begins the delicate dance
of care and protection.
Bless the weeds, plants not planted,
but deserving of life.
Bless the pigeon, the squirrel, and the butterfly
searching for their share of creation's bounty.
Teach me not to over emphasise my importance,
but to be a part of all the whole web of life.

Autumn
Praise the harvest!
Rejoice in the compost!
I see your creation
and it is good!

Bless the produce, beating all the odds
to feed my body and soul.
Bless the compost bin, teaching us
there is no such thing as waste.
Bless the microbes busy decomposing
and recomposing the stuff of life.
Keep reminding me of my place.
I praise you, I thank you, for gardens and allotments,
for parks and fields,
for their generous wisdom that keeps me.
Amen.

God of life,
It is your very nature to be merciful and just.
Forgive us when our prayers of supplication
demand only what we want, as if your desire for
the whole world could be met by satisfying
our individual cravings.
Help us to see that when the answer to our
selfish pleas is seemingly 'no',
it is not because we are forgotten, but because you
have remembered the intricate, fragile interweaving
of the whole of creation that does not revolve
around us alone.
Made in your image,
may our lives always prioritise justice,
mercy and peace,
not as our individual right but because of your
all-embracing love for the earth and all its
precious people.
Amen.

Even when the land, sea and sky are poisoned,
bless us with vision to heal our wounded earth.
Even as the missiles fly and the bullets rain,
bless those who work for peace and to rebuild trust.
Even as the vulnerable weep in poverty,
bless those who work to share the world's resources.
Even when the insults are thrown and prejudices shown,
bless any who welcome the stranger.
When we struggle to hope or feel weak in faith,
bless even our small acts of love and solidarity.
Amen.

When we are stuck,
when we are not sure how to make things different,
show us the alliance of the next step,
then give us the resolve to step out together.
And when together we have taken those first steps,
however ineffective they may feel,
however paltry the distance travelled,
provoke us to take some more.
Spur us into action, one small step at a time
and help us to keep going
because transformation is just a big word
for keeping on stepping out!
Amen.

Eternal One,
You are the God in whom we live and move and have our being.
We give you thanks for the diversity of life
inherent in your creation and within each and every last one of us,
wonderfully made in your image.
Today we particularly give you thanks for your rainbow children:
lesbian, gay, bisexual, trans, queer/questioning, intersex, asexual and more,
reflecting your love in their lives and relationships.
Your love transcends our labels and divisions,
creating one multihued humanity
from a stunning diversity.
May we always be ready to recognise you
in every person we see before us.
We ask this in all your holy names.
Amen.

Beyond philanthropy
is a vocation of protest.

Beyond good intentions
is a call to reformation.

Beyond kindness
is long-term commitment to social change.

Beyond today's action
is a resolution for continued resistance.

Beyond benevolent thoughts
is a radical call to justice.

Beckon us, Summoning God
into the world that is beyond:
beyond exploitation,
beyond compromise,
beyond imagination.

Summon us into your kingdom
beyond us,
beyond time,
beyond our wildest dreams.
Amen.

A shout for joy!
We give thanks for the air in our lungs!
We shout out for justice in this world.
We sing out gladly in solidarity with the vulnerable.
We lift our voices with all those who are in
need of hope.

If we were to stay silent,
the very stones would cry out.
We know God has seen the suffering of the people
and has heard our cries.
So, we shout for joy,
because God hears us, and we know justice is
coming.
Amen!

(Based on Luke 19:40 and Exodus 3:7)

Bless us with more determination than cynicism,
more resolve than despair,
more passion than apathy.

Bless us with restless spirits,
deep longings for justice,
resolve for equality.

Bless us with the desire for change,
wisdom to see how to realise it,
and energy to make it happen.
Amen.

Justice is an active word,
an unsettling word,
it stirs the waters of complacency,
it insists we dive in.

Grow us to recognise that
justice is a vocation,
imperative,
a calling, for God's sake
to live differently.
Amen.

Help us, Creator God,
to stand in the listening spaces,
to wait in the silent places,
to walk gently
on the earth's surface
leaving no mark
except imprints of grace.
Amen.

A Simple Pattern of Prayer

The purpose of this book is to embed our longing for justice, peace and change into our regular patterns of worship and commitment. Including additional prayers and meditations not featured earlier in We Have Voices, *below is a simple example of how you might use some of these contributions to lead worship, either on Sunday, at a housegroup or before a meeting. It is just an example and is shared here to encourage you to work imaginatively with these* We Have Voices *prayers.*

Thank you, Creator, for this day;
for a fresh start, for the breath and pulse of life within
us and around us.
Thank you, Jesus, for these people, colleagues and friends,
companions and conspirators, together in bread, together
in spirit, together aspiring to your kingdom.
Thank you, Spirit of Wisdom, for all the quirks and questions of
our lives; breathe into this gathering with insight and kindness,
let us be gracious and open, let us be surprised by beauty,
let us relish this gift of another day.

Pray through us today,
pray within us this day,
pray around us this day,
pray between us this day.
May your call on our life, always be for love.

Hymn

Reading

As we listen to the reading, let us reflect on our own vocation – where is Jesus calling us out from, what is Jesus calling us into?
Where is Jesus calling the people of the world from death to life?
How will our personal calling be part of God's calling to all people?

Pray through us today,
pray within us this day,
pray around us this day,
pray between us this day.
May your call on our life, always be for love.

If I need to be less proud, forgive me.
If I need more self-esteem, empower me.
If I need to be less greedy, forgive me.
If I need to demand a fair share, empower me.
If I have hurt or bullied others, forgive me.
If I am the victim of abuse, empower me.
If I have sought power at the expense of others, forgive me.
If I need courage to find my voice, empower me.
If I have defended my own privilege, forgive me.
If I have been too deferent, empower me.
If I have assumed my place in the kingdom of heaven, forgive me.
If I have assumed I have no place in the kingdom of heaven, empower me.
Amen.

Let us pray for people who are calling out for justice, peace, transformation and hope.

Unclench the fists of injustice, open arms of peace,
untie knots of oppressions, weave garments of reconciliation,
loosen tight lips and closed minds to sing freedom songs.
Unbind our cynicism, call us out.
Call out our inequality, our aggression and our greed.
Like Lazarus call us out,
drown out death's final word,
summon us with love's authority
into the dazzling hope of a shared and equal life.
Amen.

Hymn

Pray through us today,
pray within us this day,
pray around us this day,
pray between us this day.
May your call on our life, always be for love.

About the Editor

The Revd Dr Barbara Glasson is a Methodist minister and tutor in pastoral theology at the Queen's Foundation for Theological Education in Birmingham.

Despite growing up in Kent and gaining a first degree in Agricultural Sciences, she has worked predominantly in city centres in the north of the UK.

In 2019 she was awarded the Archbishop of Canterbury's Hubert Walter Award in recognition of her work in peace and reconciliation. She was President of the 2019/2020 Methodist Conference.

Barbara is a Churchill Fellow and has travelled widely and written a number of books that reflect her commitment to social justice and peace.

Contributors

Angie Allport
Mel Beaven
James Carver
Ashley Cooper
Sam Cree
Delyth Wyn Davies
Barbara Easton
Hilary Evans
Ellie Fearn
John Forsdick
Barbara Glasson
David Glasson
Gary Hall
Warren Hartley
Ned Hilton
Graeme Hodge
Christopher Holmes
Jim Hope
Chris Howson
Penny Johnson
Susan Jones
Rachel Lampard
Alana Lawrence
Paul Mellor
Paul Nzacahayo
Raj Bharath Patta
Romeo Pedro
Bevan Powell
Américo Jara Reyes
Richard Reddie
Mark Slaney
Sandy Sneddon
Simon Sutcliffe
Erica Taylor
Lal Din Thara
Roger Walton